Bond

10 Minute Tests

7-8 years

Sarah Lindsay

English

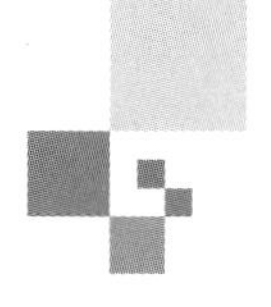

Nelson Thornes

Test 1: Mixed

Test time: 0 5 10 minutes

Underline the *collective noun* in each sentence.

1 The army marched for many miles.

2 The flock of seagulls screeched as they circled above the sea.

3 The pack worked together when out hunting.

4 The netball team won the trophy.

5 The singer cried when she was given a bunch of flowers.

Add ing to each of these words. Watch out for spelling changes!

6 plan ________________________

7 promote ________________________

8 punch ________________________

9 prance ________________________

10 punish ________________________

With a line, match each word with its *definition*.

11	excess	an organised journey
12	exchange	a way out
13	expedition	too much of something
14	excellent	very accurate
15	exact	to trade one thing for another
16	exit	very good

Write a sentence using all of the words in bold. The words must be in a list. Don't forget the commas!

e.g. **pen pencil rubber**

In my schoolbag I have a pen, a pencil and a rubber.

17 **bread rolls cakes**

____

____

18 **flute trombone drums violin**

____

____

19 **pyjamas toothbrush towel**

____

____

20 **car bus train plane**

____

____

Total

TEST 2: Spelling

Test time: 0 5 10 minutes

Write each of these words correctly.

1 skool ____________

2 tomorow ____________

3 afriad ____________

4 candl ____________

5 lasy ____________

6 dreem ____________

7 smooke ____________

8 cuaght ____________

9 streat ____________

10 cudle ____________

Add the *prefix* un or dis to make a word.

11 ____________obey

12 ____________count

13 ____________happy

14 ____________trust

15 ____________appear

16 ____________dress

17 ____________wise

18 ____________tidy

Circle the silent letter in each word.

19 w r i g g l e

20 k n e e

21 k n i g h t

22 t h u m b

23 k n o c k

24 c o m b

25 w r i t e

Total

Test 3: Spelling

Test time: 0 5 10 minutes

Underline the *root word* in each of these words.

1 c h e e r f u l

2 f a i r l y

3 f r i e n d s h i p

4 p e a c e f u l

5 u s e l e s s

6 q u i e t e s t

7 h e l p l e s s

8 c l o u d y

Put a tick next to the words spelled correctly and a cross next to those spelled incorrectly.

9 stoped ☐

10 diffrent ☐

11 together ☐

12 openned ☐

13 whatch ☐

14 suddenly ☐

15 inportant ☐

16 always ☐

17 found ☐

18 clothes ☐

Add the *suffix* to each word. Don't forget any spelling changes!

19 quick + est ____________________

20 close + er ____________________

21 thin + est ____________________

22 nice + er ____________________

23 long + est ____________________

24 funny + er ____________________

25 tall + est ____________________

Total

Test 4: Comprehension

Test time: 0 5 10 minutes

Read this letter carefully.

54 Devon Place
Trewince
Nr Truro
Cornwall
TR4 9EF

4th October

Dear Tanya

How are things at school? Has Mrs Cooper kept you all in for talking too much yet?

Our new house is great. I have my own room, which Mum and Dad have painted pink. They bought me one of those beds with a desk underneath it and a beanbag so my friends have somewhere to sit. I'd love you to come and stay sometime. Najib also has his own room but it isn't as nice as mine!

The garden is much bigger than our old one. There is a tree house at the bottom of the garden, but at the moment the stepladder is broken so it's really hard getting into it. I have to stand on Najib's shoulders! There is also a stream nearby where we go with our nets. I caught a fish yesterday. We don't watch as much television these days as there is so much to play with and do outside.

There is one big problem though. I haven't found any real friends to play with. It makes me wish I was back in Stafford, going to school with you. I miss Gable Primary School so much. The people in my class are OK and talk to me sometimes but I feel so lonely because they never ask me to play with them. How are they going to know if they like me if they don't ask me to play with them sometimes?

Please come and stay soon, we would have great fun.

Missing you.

Anneena

Answer these questions about the letter.

1 On which date did Anneena write this letter?

____

2 What is special about Anneena's new bed?

____

3 What is the name of Anneena's brother?

____

4 What is the problem with the tree house?

____

5 Why doesn't Anneena watch television as much as she used to?

____

____

6 Where did Anneena's family live before they moved to Cornwall?

____

7 How do we know Anneena is feeling unhappy?

____

____

8 What would you write to Anneena to make her feel better?

____

____

____

Time for a break! Go to Puzzle Page 38

Total

Test 5: **Vocabulary**

Test time: 0 5 10 minutes

Draw a line to match the *antonyms*.

1	never	freeze
2	happy	before
3	boil	always
4	pack	sad
5	after	unpack

Write two sentences for each word. In each sentence the word must have a different meaning.

6–7 tear

(1) ______________________________

____

(2) ______________________________

____

8–9 match

(1) ______________________________

____

(2) ______________________________

____

Write these words in *alphabetical order*.

seagull fly donkey fox snail

10 (1) ______________________________

11 (2) ______________________________

12 (3) ______________________________

13 (4) ______________________________

14 (5) ______________________________

Write the expressions in the table.

15–20 Must go! Mind the step!

Watch out! See you later!

Farewell! Careful!

Expression of warning	Expression of leaving

Total

Test 6: **Mixed**

Test time: 0 5 10 minutes

Underline the two words in each line that have similar meanings.

1	kind	nasty	mean
2	starving	hungry	bloated
3	jump	trip	leap
4	funny	comical	appealing
5	new	tattered	shabby

Complete the table by placing the *pronouns* in the correct box.

6–11 she them his him they her

Plural	Female	Male

Circle the *compound words*.

12–16

cupboard	queen	checkout
wheel	snowdrop	stereo
elephant	weekend	flower
computer	football	towel

Copy these sentences, adding the missing capital letters.

17 have you read the tracy beaker books?

____

____

18 let's meet up at the park on saturday.

____

____

19 we are visiting warwick castle in june.

____

____

20 can nazar come to daniel's birthday party?

____

____

Total

Test 7: Grammar

Test time: 0 5 10 minutes

Rewrite the *proper nouns* in this passage correctly.

1–5 The spaceship left in july and was due to land on mars in a couple of days. Henry had entered his school's competition to talk to the astronauts, not really believing he might win. Now the astronaut, sid jenkins, was here in dovedale, talking to him about what he had for breakfast!

____

____

____

____

____

Underline the *singular nouns* and circle the *plural nouns*.

6 engines

7 chief

8 dwarfs

9 children

10 holiday

With a line, match the present and past *tenses* of these *verbs*.

11	throw	was
12	swing	took
13	is	went
14	go	swung
15	take	threw

Choose the most appropriate *adjective* to fill each space. Each *adjective* may be used only once.

strong   curly   playful   thick   comfortable

16 ______________________________ book

17 ______________________________ hair

18 ______________________________ rabbit

19 ______________________________ wind

20 ______________________________ bed

Total

Test time: 0 5 10 minutes

Read this extract carefully.

The Wizard of Oz *by L. Frank Baum*

1 *Dorothy and her little dog, Toto, are blown by a tornado into a magical world. To get back to her world, Dorothy has to travel down the yellow brick road to the Wizard. On her journey she meets some interesting characters who want to travel with her.*

When Dorothy awoke the sun was
5 shining through the trees and Toto had long been out chasing birds around her. There was the scarecrow, still standing patiently in the corner, waiting for her.

"We must go and search for water,"
10 she said to him.

"Why do you want water?" he asked.

"To wash my face clean after the dust of the road, and to drink, so the bread will not stick in my throat."

15 "It must be inconvenient to be made of flesh," said the Scarecrow, thoughtfully, "for you must sleep, and eat and drink. However you have brains, and it is worth a lot of bother to be able to think
20 properly."

They left the cottage and walked through the trees until they found a little spring of clear water, where Dorothy drank and bathed and ate her
25 breakfast. She saw there was not much bread left in the basket, and the girl was thankful the Scarecrow did not have to eat anything, for there was scarcely enough for herself and Toto for the day.

30 When she had finished her meal, and was about to go back to the road of yellow brick, she was startled to hear a deep groan near by.

"What was that?" she asked timidly.

35 "I cannot imagine," replied the Scarecrow; "but we can go and see."

Just then another groan reached their ears, and the sound seemed to come from behind them. They turned and walked
40 through the forest a few steps, when Dorothy discovered something shining in a ray of sunshine that fell between the trees. She ran to the place and then stopped short, with a cry of surprise.

45 One of the big trees had been partly chopped through, and standing beside it, with an uplifted axe in his hands, was a man made entirely of tin...

Answer these questions about the extract.

1 Who is Toto?

___

2 Who was waiting for Dorothy when she awoke?

___

3 Why did Dorothy need water?

___

4 What did the Scarecrow eat?

___

5 What colour was the road Dorothy was following?

___

6 What does the word '**inconvenient**' on line 15 mean?

___

7 What first alerted Dorothy and the Scarecrow that there was something in the trees?

___

8 How do you think Dorothy felt on discovering the man made of tin? Why?

___

___

___

Time for a break! Go to Puzzle Page 39

Total

Test 9: **Mixed**

Test time: 0 5 10 minutes

Complete the missing punctuation at the end of each *phrase* or sentence.

1 The spider wondered where best to spin its web ___

2 What tune shall I play next ___

3 Delicious ___

4 Isn't it time we went to catch the train ___

5 My house is the second on the right ___

Write three sentences with each one including a *pronoun* and a *verb*.

6–7 ______________________________

____

8–9 ______________________________

____

10–11 ______________________________

____

Write these words in *alphabetical order*.

stack swivel sprain subtract squirt

12 (1) ______________________

13 (2) ______________________

14 (3) ______________________

15 (4) ______________________

16 (5) ______________________

Read the clues to help find the words ending in le.

17 It opens a door. ha______________

18 a shape with four sides rec______________

19 to break into small pieces cr______________

20 one s______________

Total

TEST 10: Spelling

Test time: 0 5 10 minutes

Add the missing apostrophes (').

1 was not = w a s n t

2 you will = y o u l l

3 we have = w e v e

4 she is = s h e s

5 could not = c o u l d n t

6 I have = I v e

7 they had = t h e y d

Write each of these *nouns* in their *plural* form.

8 display ____________________

9 pond ____________________

10 fox ____________________

11 desk ____________________

12 party ____________________

13 table ____________________

14 shoe ____________________

15 sandwich ____________________

Circle the correct spelling of each word.

16	nowere	nowhere
17	study	studie
18	beautiful	beautful
19	rescuw	rescue
20	migt	might
21	upstiars	upstairs
22	autumn	autum
23	scramble	scrambel
24	bruther	brother
25	February	Febuary

Total

TEST 11: Spelling

Test time: 0 5 10 minutes

All these words have a silent letter missing. Write each word correctly.

1 rong ____________

2 nickers ____________

3 nife ____________

4 crum ____________

5 samon ____________

6 dout ____________

7 wale ____________

8 onest ____________

9 reck ____________

10 neel ____________

Add ing to each of these words. Watch out for spelling changes!

11 spend ____________

12 enjoy ____________

13 ride ____________

14 meet ____________

15 care ____________

16 rub ____________

17 clap ____________

18 smile ____________

Add the *suffixes* ly or ful to each of these to make a word.

19 pain____________

20 week____________

21 forget____________

22 wonder____________

23 friend____________

24 hope____________

25 stupid____________

Total

Test 12: Sentences

Test time: 0 5 10 minutes

Copy and add the missing speech marks to these sentences.

1 Shall we go outside on the trampoline? asked Orrin.

____

____

2 I wish we didn't have so much homework, exclaimed Jake.

____

____

3 I can't wait to go riding after school, said Jane excitedly.

____

____

4 Oh no, I've forgotten my swimming things! moaned India.

____

____

Add the missing exclamation marks (!) or question marks (?) where they are needed.

5 Watch out ______

6 Where is my coat ______

7 Quick, run ______

8 Has the rain stopped yet ______

9 Do you think we should go on our own ______

10 I love it ______

Add the missing commas to these sentences.

11–12 I must not forget my hat scarf coat and boots.

13 During the spring we had a robin nest in the shed blue-tits in the bird box and starlings in the tree.

14 Dad has bought Mum a necklace some earrings and a new watch for her birthday.

15–16 Nan needs apples oranges chicken and bread from the shop.

Finish these sentences in your own words.

17 I swam to him but ______________________________

____

18 Aimee had been holding her mum's hand but ______________________________

____

19 The spaceship landed with a jolt and ______________________________

____

20 The postman tripped as ______________________________

____

Test time: 0 5 10 minutes

Read this poem carefully.

The Cow *by Robert Louis Stevenson*

1 The friendly cow all red and white,
I love with all my heart:
She gives me cream with all her might,
To eat with apple tart.

5 She wanders lowing here and there,
And yet she cannot stray
All in the pleasant open air,
The pleasant light of day;

And blown by all the winds that pass
10 And wet with all the showers,
She walks among the meadow grass
And eats the meadow flowers.

Answers

Answers will vary for questions that require children to answer in their own words. Possible answers to most of these questions are given in *italics*.

Test 1: Mixed

1 The army marched for many miles.
2 The flock of seagulls screeched as they circled above the sea.
3 The pack worked together when out hunting.
4 The netball team won the trophy.
5 The singer cried when she was given a bunch of flowers.
6 planning
7 promoting
8 punching
9 prancing
10 punishing
11 excess – too much of something
12 exchange – to trade one thing for another
13 expedition – an organised journey
14 excellent – very good
15 exact – very accurate
16 exit – a way out
17–20 *Four sentences, each using the words in bold in a list showing the correct use of commas, e.g. Mum asked me to buy bread, rolls and some cakes from the bakery.*

Test 2: Spelling

1 school
2 tomorrow
3 afraid
4 candle
5 lazy
6 dream
7 smoke
8 caught
9 street
10 cuddle
11 disobey
12 discount
13 unhappy
14 distrust
15 disappear
16 undress
17 unwise
18 untidy
19 wriggle
20 knee
21 knight
22 thumb
23 knock
24 comb
25 write

Test 3: Spelling

1 cheerful
2 fairly
3 friendship
4 peaceful
5 useless
6 quietest
7 helpless
8 cloudy
9 ✗
10 ✗
11 ✓
12 ✗
13 ✗
14 ✓
15 ✗
16 ✓
17 ✓
18 ✓
19 quickest
20 closer
21 thinnest
22 nicer
23 longest
24 funnier
25 tallest

Test 4: Comprehension

1 Anneena wrote the letter on 4th October.
2 Anneena's bed has a desk beneath it.
3 Anneena's brother is called Najib.
4 The ladder up to the tree house is broken.
5 Anneena doesn't watch as much television as she used to because there is so much she can play with and do outside.
6 Anneena's family lived in Stafford.
7 Anneena writes about how she misses her old school and her friend, Tanya, and about not having made any good friends yet which is making her lonely.
8 *I would tell her that I missed her and remind her that it might take a bit longer but that soon she'd have lots of friends.*

Test 5: Vocabulary

1 never – always
2 happy – sad
3 boil – freeze
4 pack – unpack
5 after – before
6–7 *I got a tear in my trousers when I played football at lunch. A tear fell from her cheek when they said goodbye to her parents.*
8–9 *We couldn't have a campfire because we didn't have a match to light the fire. They played the football match in the rain.*
10 donkey
11 fly
12 fox
13 seagull
14 snail
15–20

Expression of warning	Expression of leaving
Mind the step!	Must go!
Watch out!	See you later!
Careful!	Farewell!

Test 6: Mixed

1 nasty, mean
2 starving, hungry
3 jump, leap
4 funny, comical
5 tattered, shabby
6–11

Plural	Female	Male
them	she	his
they	her	him

12–16 cupboard, checkout, snowdrop, weekend, football
17 Have you read the Tracy Beaker books?
18 Let's meet up at the park on Saturday.
19 We are visiting Warwick Castle in June.
20 Can Nazar come to Daniel's birthday party?

Test 7: Grammar

1–5 July, Mars, Sid Jenkins, Dovedale
6 engines
7 chief
8 dwarfs
9 children
10 holiday
11 throw – threw
12 swing – swung
13 is – was
14 go – went
15 take – took
16 thick
17 curly
18 playful
19 strong
20 comfortable

Test 8: Comprehension

1 Toto is Dorothy's little dog.
2 The Scarecrow was waiting for Dorothy when she awoke.
3 Dorothy needed water to wash her face and to drink.
4 The Scarecrow didn't eat anything.
5 The road Dorothy was following was yellow.
6 *'Inconvenient' means awkward, troublesome or difficult.*
7 Dorothy and the Scarecrow heard a groan near by.
8 *I think Dorothy felt surprised because in her world there weren't any people made of tin.*

Test 9: Mixed

1 .
2 ?
3 !
4 ?
5 .
6–11 *We climbed the ladder to the tree house then ate our lunch.*
12 sprain
13 squirt
14 stack
15 subtract
16 swivel
17 handle
18 rectangle
19 crumble
20 single

Test 10: Spelling

1 wasn't
2 you'll
3 we've
4 she's
5 couldn't
6 I've
7 they'd
8 displays
9 ponds
10 foxes
11 desks
12 parties
13 tables
14 shoes
15 sandwiches
16 nowhere
17 study
18 beautiful
19 rescue
20 might
21 upstairs
22 autumn
23 scramble
24 brother
25 February

Test 11: Spelling

1 wrong
2 knickers
3 knife
4 crumb
5 salmon
6 doubt
7 whale
8 honest
9 wreck
10 kneel
11 spending
12 enjoying
13 riding
14 meeting
15 caring
16 rubbing
17 clapping
18 smiling
19 painful
20 weekly
21 forgetful
22 wonderful
23 friendly
24 hopeful
25 stupidly

Test 12: Sentences

1 "Shall we go outside on the trampoline?" asked Orrin.
2 "I wish we didn't have so much homework," exclaimed Jake.
3 "I can't wait to go riding after school," said Jane excitedly.
4 "Oh no, I've forgotten my swimming things!" moaned India.

5 !
6 ?
7 !
8 ?
9 ?
10 !
11–12 I must not forget my hat**,** scarf**,** coat and boots.
13 During the spring we had a robin nest in the shed**,** blue-tits in the bird box and starlings in the tree.
14 Dad has bought Mum a necklace**,** some earrings and a new watch for her birthday.
15–16 Nan needs apples**,** oranges**,** chicken and bread from the shop.
17 I swam to him but *couldn't get there in time to get the ball.*
18 Aimee had been holding her mum's hand but *suddenly it wasn't there and she felt scared.*
19 The spaceship landed with a jolt and *a strange group of creatures began climbing from its windows.*
20 The postman tripped as *he ran from the barking dog.*

Test 13: Comprehension

1 The cow is red and white.
2 Cream is eaten with apple tart.
3 'day' rhymes with 'stray'
4 Windy and showery weather is mentioned in the third verse.
5 The cow enjoys eating meadow flowers.
6 'light of day' (line 8)
7 In the second line the poet says that he loves the cow with all his heart.
8 *Yes, because he writes nice things about the outdoors, such as 'the pleasant open air'.*

Test 14: Mixed

1–3 *I like to watch swimming on telly. Are you trying out for the school play? Run, there's a werewolf following us!*
4 *happy*
5 *multiply*
6 *sip*
7 *fall*
8 *walk*
9 *leave*
10 class
11 wife
12 bike
13 circle
14 fly
15 scarf
16–20 Wembley Stadium, Prince William, Saturn, Sunday, Lucy

Test 15: Vocabulary

1 whiteboard
2 clipboard
3 nowhere
4 thumbnail
5 paintbrush
6 raindrop
7 anywhere
8 dull, boring
9 sprint, run
10 steal, rob
11 gently, carefully
12 pineapple
13 plum
14 prune
15 pumpkin
16 hazard – something that could harm you
17 loch – a Scottish lake or inlet
18 sculpture – an object made by an artist
19 carnival – a party or procession in the streets
20 mane – long, thick hair that grows from the neck

Test 16: Mixed

1 ear
2 use
3 den
4 one
5 are
6 **"**Please can I have some sweets?**"** asked Tina.
7 Raef called, **"**Bet I beat you to the swings!**"**
8 **"**I wish we had football practice today,**"** moaned Joe.
9 **"**Sing loudly and clearly,**"** shouted the teacher.
10 (gnawed)
11 (guest)
12 (hour)
13 (wrapped)
14 (climber)
15 The smooth, brown snake hid behind the rock.
16 The bird flapped its strong wings.
17 Monty the dog leapt the broken fence.
18 The loud music could be heard across the busy street.
19 As the wind whipped around the corner the clay pot was knocked over.
20 Mia's long, thick hair is often tied in bunches.

Test 17: Grammar

1 yet
2 but
3 so
4 although
5–10 *E.g. The spooky house stood alone on the hill.*
11–15 colony, herd, group, pack, litter
16 *fell*
17 *Run*
18 *followed*
19 *sped*
20 *fell*

Test 18: Comprehension

1 Smell is the stronger sense.
2 Scent particles go into our noses to help us smell.
3 Most people can recognise about 3,000 smells.
4 The messages from the nose and tongue are sent to the brain.
5 We taste sour things at the sides of our tongue.
6 *We sneeze to help clean out our noses of particles that aren't wanted.*
7 *It is important to cover our noses with our hands when we sneeze as the air coming out of our mouths is travelling so fast it can easily spread germs.*
8 Child's own question e.g. *Why do I sometimes feel like I'm going to sneeze, but I don't?*

Test 19: Mixed

1 *She needs to get dressed.*
2 *He hates eating rhubarb.*
3 *She feels very tired.*
4 *He nearly drowned.*
5 "You must feed your rabbit, George," reminded Mum.
6 "Quick! I've got to get home," yelled Alex.
7 "I think it might rain," moaned Rupa.
8 Kim giggled, "Mum has forgotten to brush her hair!"
9 Coco cried, "But it isn't fair!"
10 tested
11 amusing
12 dropped
13 hiding
14 cancelled
15–16 swallow – *a type of bird; food moving down the throat*
17–18 seal – *a sea animal, a covering fixed around an edge to stop leaking; a mark that is put or stamped on something*
19–20 right – *correct; the opposite to left*

Test 20: Sentences

1 ?
2 ?
3 .
4 ! .
5 .
6 The Wedding Ghost
7 How Science Works
8 Gobbolino the Witch's Cat
9 The BFG
10 Scary Stories for Eight Year Olds
11 "Can we go to Lambing Day at Hope Farm**?**" asked Lola.
12 Mrs Cantillon screamed, "Be careful**!**"
13 "Whose birthday is it this week**?**" the headteacher asked.
14 Hannah called, "Are you coming to the park**?**"
15 **"**Don't eat all the sweets or you might be sick," Mum laughed.
16 "Time for bed I'm afraid**,**" said the babysitter.
17 Harry Potter was Josh's favourite character.
18 On Thursday Sarah has been invited to a sleepover.
19 The Stamp family walked from Bohortha to Towan Beach.
20 We had to go to Safebury's but on the way home Mum took us to Burger Queen.

Puzzle 1

dog
knife
Tina
chicken
weight
gloves

Puzzle 2

jumping, waving, lovely, smartly, powerful, doubtful, happiness, hopeless

Puzzle 3

in, or, for, form, mat, at, on, format, formation, inform, info, ion, ma

Puzzle 4

below
Earth
money
swimming
year
white
watch
first

Puzzle 5

Child's own answers, e.g. *the brown bear; the fast muddy bike*

Answer these questions about the poem.

1 What colour is the cow?

___

2 What is eaten with the apple tart?

___

3 Find a word in the poem rhyming with '**stray**'.

___

4 List two types of weather mentioned in the third verse.

___

5 Which flowers does the cow enjoy eating?

___

6 Which phrase in the poem means '**daylight**'?

___

7 Which line in the poem tells us the poet loves this cow?

___

8 Do you think the poet enjoys life outdoors? Why?

___

___

___

Total

Test 14: **Mixed**

Test time: 0 5 10 minutes

Write three sentences. End one sentence with a full stop, one with a question mark and one with an exclamation mark.

1 ______________________________

____

2 ______________________________

____

3 ______________________________

____

Write an *antonym* for each of these words.

4 miserable ____________________

5 divide ____________________

6 gulp ____________________

7 rise ____________________

8 run ____________________

9 arrive ____________________

Change each of these words from *plural* to *singular*.

10 classes ______________________

11 wives ______________________

12 bikes ______________________

13 circles ______________________

14 flies ______________________

15 scarves ______________________

Circle the *proper nouns* and then write them using the correct capital letters.

16–20 wembley stadium snowman

yellow prince william

saturn sunday

elbow lucy

______________________ ______________________ ______________________

______________________ ______________________

Test 15: Vocabulary

Test time: 0 5 10 minutes

Write a *compound word* by adding one of the words in the box to each of the words below. You will need to use some words from the box more than once.

nail	drop	brush	where	board

1 white ____________________

2 clip ____________________

3 no ____________________

4 thumb ____________________

5 paint ____________________

6 rain ____________________

7 any ____________________

Underline the two words on each line that are *synonyms*.

8	dull	cruel	boring
9	crawl	sprint	run
10	steal	buy	rob
11	gently	busily	carefully

Write these words in *alphabetical order*.

prune plum pumpkin pineapple

12 (1) ______________

13 (2) ______________

14 (3) ______________

15 (4) ______________

Use a line to match each word with its *definition*.

16	hazard	a Scottish lake or inlet
17	loch	a party or procession in the streets
18	sculpture	long, thick hair that grows from the neck
19	carnival	something that could harm you
20	mane	an object made by an artist

Total

Test 16: **Mixed**

Test time: 0 5 10 minutes

Write one small word you can find in each of these words that is three letters long. The letters in each word must remain in the same order.

e.g. course — *our*

1 heard ________

2 because ________

3 gardener ________

4 money ________

5 share ________

Copy and add the missing speech marks to these sentences.

6 Please can I have some sweets? asked Tina.

____

____

7 Raef called, Bet I beat you to the swings!

____

____

8 I wish we had football practice today, moaned Joe.

____

____

9 Sing loudly and clearly, shouted the teacher.

____

____

Circle the word in each sentence that has a silent letter.

10 The rabbit gnawed at the branch.

11 We have a guest visiting us this weekend.

12 Jane's swimming lesson lasted for an hour.

13 The chicken's wing wrapped around the new-born chick.

14 The climber was scared by a nesting seagull.

Underline the *adjective* or *adjectives* in each sentence.

15 The smooth, brown snake hid behind the rock.

16 The bird flapped its strong wings.

17 Monty the dog leapt the broken fence.

18 The loud music could be heard across the busy street.

19 As the wind whipped around the corner the clay pot was knocked over.

20 Mia's long, thick hair is often tied in bunches.

Time for a break! Go to Puzzle Page 41

Total

TEST 17: **Grammar**

Test time: 0 5 10 minutes

Underline all the *connectives* in each of these sentences.

1 I saw Jemma lick my ice cream yet she said she didn't!

2 Jacob said the blue toy car was his but I found it in a bush.

3 Kate and I ride our bikes so we won't be late for gym club.

4 Mr Gallop told us to put the footballs away, although they were very wet.

Write three sentences, each containing a *noun* and an *adjective*.

5–6 ______________________________

____

7–8 ______________________________

____

9–10 ______________________________

____

Circle the *collective nouns*.

11–15

dog	London	colony
herd	mountain	Tuesday
group	calculator	pack
Ellie	Saturn	litter

Fill each gap with a *verb*.

16 Poppy ______________ from the barn roof and hurt herself.

17 ______________ or we will be late!

18 The chicks ______________ their mother everywhere.

19 The old lady ______________ round the shops on her buggy.

20 Taylor ______________ and broke his arm.

Total

Read this information carefully.

Smell and taste

Smell and taste are important senses. Our sense of smell is much stronger than our sense of taste. When we taste food, we rely on its smell and texture to give us information about it as well.

We use our noses for smelling things. Tiny scent particles go into the nose with the air. The nose then sends messages through a nerve to the brain, which recognises the smell. Most people can identify about 3,000 different smells.

The tongue also sends nerve signals to the brain about tastes. When we eat something, the tongue and the nose combine to let the brain know all about the food.

We taste different things on different parts of the tongue. We taste sweet things at the tip, salty things just behind the tip, sour things at the sides, and bitter things at the back of the tongue.

Why do we sneeze?

We sneeze to help clear our noses of unwanted particles, such as dust. When we sneeze, the rush of air from the lungs can reach a speed of 160 km/h – as fast as a sports car.

Tasting with our tongue

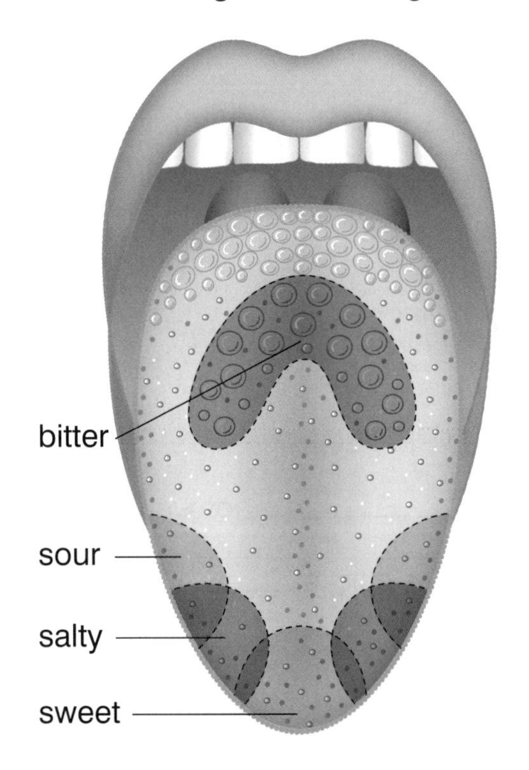

Answer these questions about the extract.

1 Which sense is stronger, smell or taste?

___

2 What goes into our noses with air to help us smell things?

___

3 How many smells can most people recognise?

___

4 Where are the messages from the nose and tongue sent?

___

5 Where on the tongue do we taste sour things?

___

6 In your own words, write why we sneeze.

___

___

7 Why do you think it is important to put our hands over our noses when we sneeze?

___

___

8 Write a question about ‘smell and taste’ that you would like to know the answer to and that isn’t answered in the passage.

___

___

Total

Test 19: Mixed

Test time: 0 5 10 minutes

Rewrite each sentence as if you are writing about someone else.

e.g. I love walking the dog. *He loves walking the dog.*

1 I need to get dressed.

____

2 I hate eating rhubarb.

____

3 I feel very tired.

____

4 I nearly drowned.

____

Underline the words that are spoken.

5 "You must feed your rabbit, George," reminded Mum.

6 "Quick! I've got to get home," yelled Alex.

7 "I think it might rain," moaned Rupa.

8 Kim giggled, "Mum has forgotten to brush her hair!"

9 Coco cried, "But it isn't fair!"

Add the *suffix* to each word. Don't forget any spelling changes!

10 test + ed = ______________________

11 amuse + ing = ______________________

12 drop + ed = ______________________

13 hide + ing = ______________________

14 cancel + ed = ______________________

Write two *definitions* for each of these words.

15–16 swallow

(1) ____

(2) ____

17–18 seal

(1) ____

(2) ____

19–20 right

(1) ____

(2) ____

Total

Test 20: Sentences

Test time: 0 5 10 minutes

Add the missing punctuation to each sentence.

1 Who won the race__

2 Isn't that your coat, Jacob__

3 The policeman enjoyed his job__

4 Watch out __ The rocks are very slippery__

5 The fire spread quickly despite the firemen soaking the ground__

Rewrite these book titles using the correct capital letters.

6 the wedding ghost

____

7 how science works

____

8 gobbolino the witch's cat

____

9 the bfg

____

10 scary stories for eight year olds

____

Add the missing punctuation mark to each of these sentences.

11 “Can we go to Lambing Day at Hope Farm ” asked Lola.

12 Mrs Cantillon screamed, “Be careful ”

13 “Whose birthday is it this week ” the headteacher asked.

14 Hannah called, “Are you coming to the park ”

15 Don’t eat all the sweets or you might be sick,” Mum laughed.

16 “Time for bed I’m afraid ” said the babysitter.

Copy these sentences, adding the missing capital letters.

17 harry potter was josh’s favourite character.

____

____

18 on thursday sarah has been invited to a sleepover.

____

____

19 the stamp family walked from bohortha to towan beach.

____

____

20 we had to go to safebury’s but on the way home Mum took us to burger queen.

____

____

Time for a break! Go to Puzzle Page 42

Total

Puzzle 1

Spot the odd word out!

Circle the word that doesn't fit.

cereal
knife
milk
toast

chick
foal
dog
kitten

chicken
sheep
goat
cow

Tom
Tim
Todd
Tina

gloves
socks
shoes
slippers

weight
grams
kilos
milligrams

Write your own list of four words with one odd one out!

Try your puzzle on someone.

__________ __________ __________ __________

Answer

Puzzle ❷

There are eight words hidden in this wordsearch that have a *suffix*.
In the boxes below, write each word that has a *suffix*.
Watch out! Not all the words in the wordsearch have *suffixes*.

p	d	o	u	b	t	f	u	l
o	p	i	f	y	d	s	l	h
w	r	i	g	g	y	t	y	o
e	s	r	w	l	p	f	l	p
r	d	g	e	b	g	r	t	e
f	k	v	s	n	k	e	r	l
u	o	a	i	r	n	s	a	e
l	t	v	k	i	d	g	m	s
h	a	p	p	i	n	e	s	s
w	b	a	d	g	r	a	p	e
n	j	u	m	p	i	n	g	e
s	b	s	m	a	o	t	l	y

Puzzle 3

Find as many smaller words as you can in this word.

information

Rules:

1 The letters have to stay in the same order and must lie next to each other, e.g. *for*.

2 Each word must have at least two letters.

Write your answers in the space below.

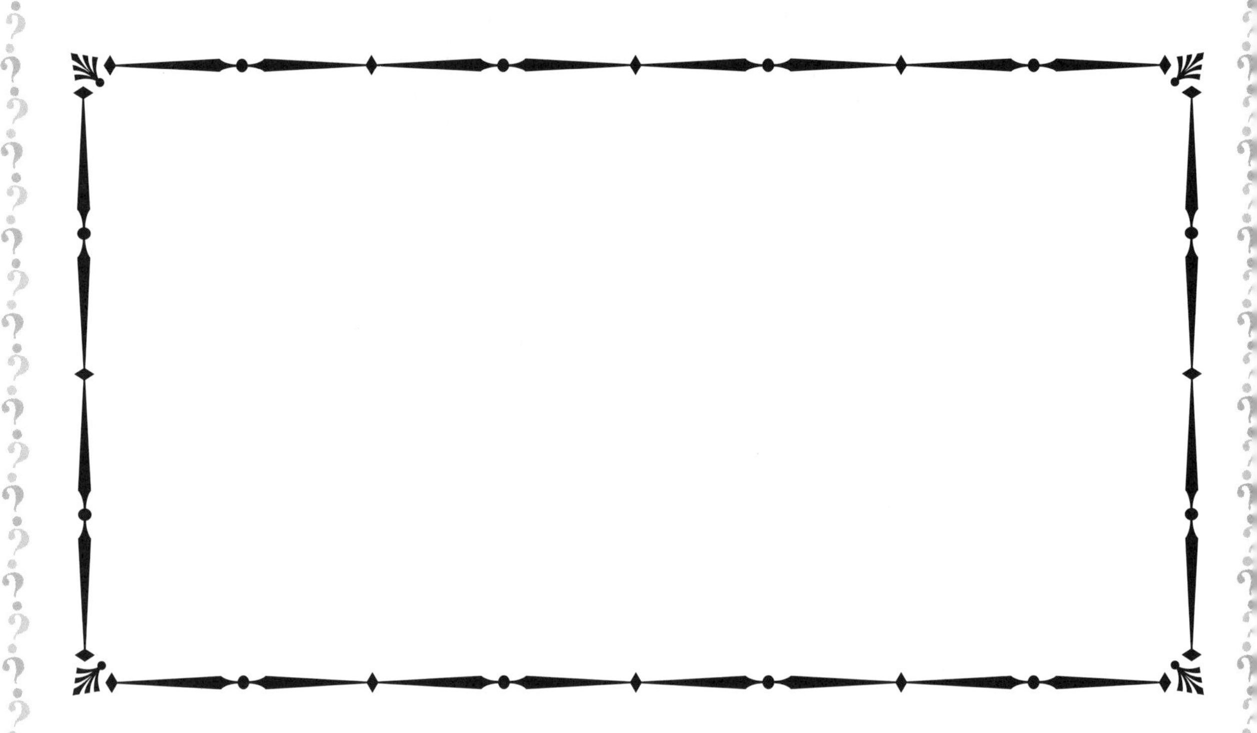

4 words = OK

6 words = good

8 words = great

9 or more words = FANTASTIC!

Puzzle 4

Find the words!

The clues will help.

- opposite to above b ____ ____ ____ ____
- the planet we live on E ____ ____ ____ ____
- used to buy things m ____ ____ ____ ____
- a fun activity in water s ____ ____ ____ ____ ____ ____ ____
- 365 days or 12 months y ____ ____ ____
- a colour w ____ ____ ____ ____
- tells the time w ____ ____ ____ ____
- opposite to last f ____ ____ ____ ____

Puzzle 5

Add a *noun* to each of these *adjectives*.

the brown ________________

the cuddly ________________

a strong ________________

some colourful ________________

a few scary ________________

Add two *adjectives* to describe each of these *nouns.*

the ________________ ________________ bike

a ________________ ________________ football

some ________________ ________________ sweets

the ________________ ________________ bus

a ________________ ________________ chick

Key words

Some special words are used in this book. You will find them picked out in *italics*. These words are explained here.

adjective	a word that describes somebody or something
alphabetical order	words arranged in the order of the letters in the alphabet
antonym	a word with a meaning opposite to another word, e.g. hot/cold
collective noun	a word referring to a group of things, e.g. a *swarm* of bees
compound word	a word made up of two other words, e.g. football
connective	a word or words that join clauses or sentences, e.g. and
definition	the meaning of a word
noun	a naming word for a person, place, feeling or thing
phrase	a group of words that act as a unit
plural	more than one, e.g. cats
prefix	a group of letters added to the beginning of a word, e.g. un, dis
pronoun	a word that can be used instead of a noun, e.g. his
proper noun	the specific name or title of a person or a place, e.g. Ben, London
root word	a word to which a prefix or suffix can be added to make another word, e.g. quick – *quick*ly
singular	one of something, e.g. cat
suffix	a group of letters added to the end of a word, e.g. ly, ful
synonym	a word with a very similar meaning to another word, e.g. quick/fast
tense	tells when an action was done, e.g. past *(I slept)*, present *(I am sleeping)* or future *(I will sleep)*
verb	a 'doing' or 'being' word

Progress Grid

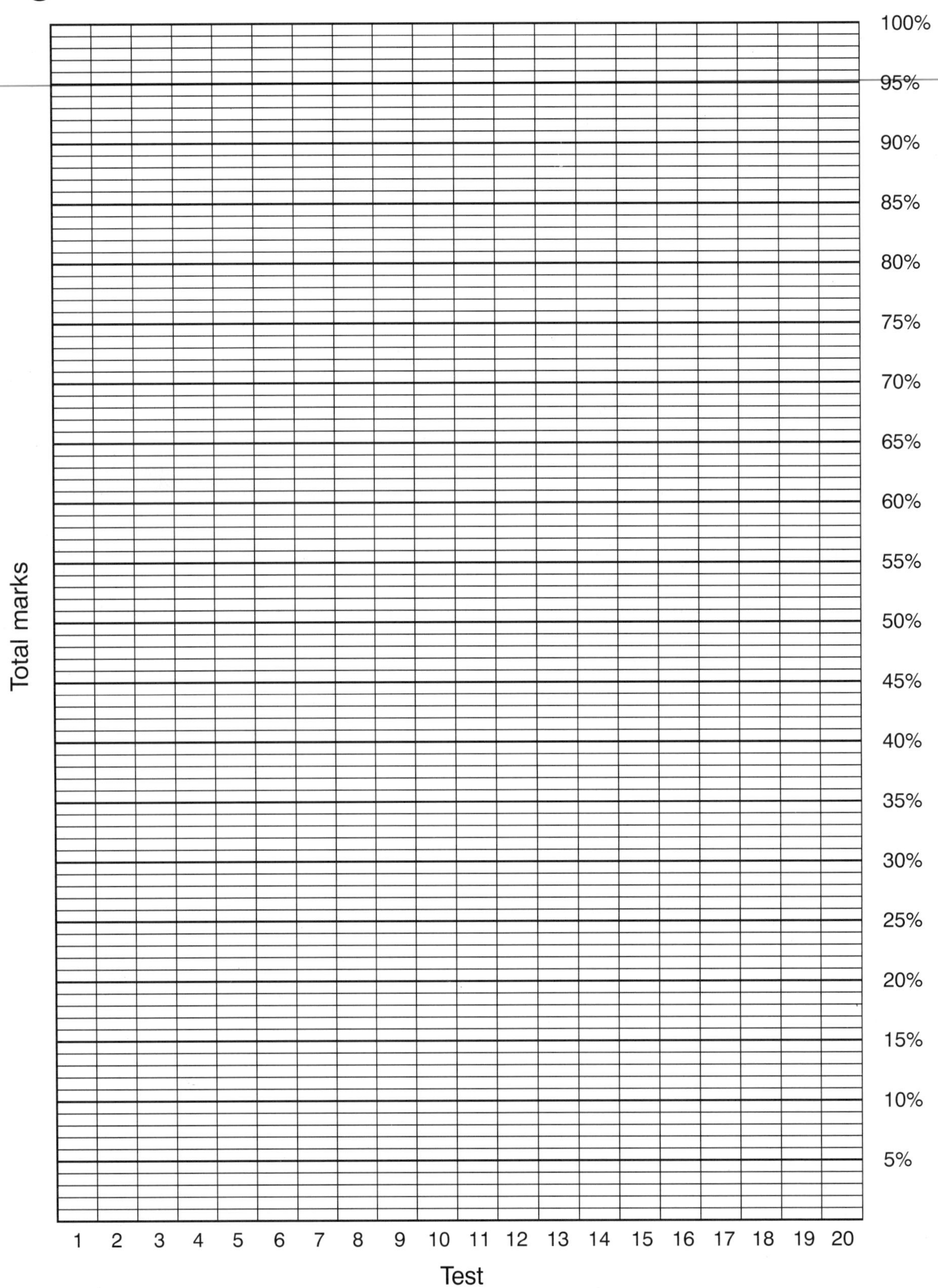